For Marie
Christmas 1975
Grandma and Grandpa Hetzel

A FIREFLY IN A FIR TREE

by Hilary Knight

HARPER & ROW, PUBLISHERS
New York, Evanston, and London

A FIREFLY IN A FIR TREE
Copyright © 1963 by Hilary Knight
Printed in the United States of America.
All rights reserved.
Library of Congress catalog card number: 63-18904

a firefly in a fir tree.

2 silver pins...

...and
a firefly in a fir tree.

On the

3rd

day of Christmas
my true love gave
to me...................

3 thistle dusters...

...two silver pins and a firefly in a fir tree.

4 holly berries...

...three thistle dusters
two silver pins and
a firefly in a fir tree.

On the

5th

day of Christmas
my true love gave
to me..................

5 bluebells...

...four holly berries
three thistle dusters
two silver pins and
a firefly in a fir tree.

6 wrens a-nesting...

...five bluebells
four holly berries
three thistle dusters
two silver pins and
a firefly in a fir tree.

7 spiders spinning...

...six wrens a-nesting
five bluebells
four holly berries
three thistle dusters
two silver pins and
a firefly in a fir tree.

8 crickets singing...

...seven spiders spinning
six wrens a-nesting
five bluebells
four holly berries
three thistle dusters
two silver pins and
a firefly in a fir tree.

9 nuts for nibbling...

...eight crickets singing
seven spiders spinning
six wrens a-nesting
five bluebells
four holly berries
three thistle dusters
two silver pins and
a firefly in a fir tree.

On the

10th

day of Christmas
my true love gave
to me...................

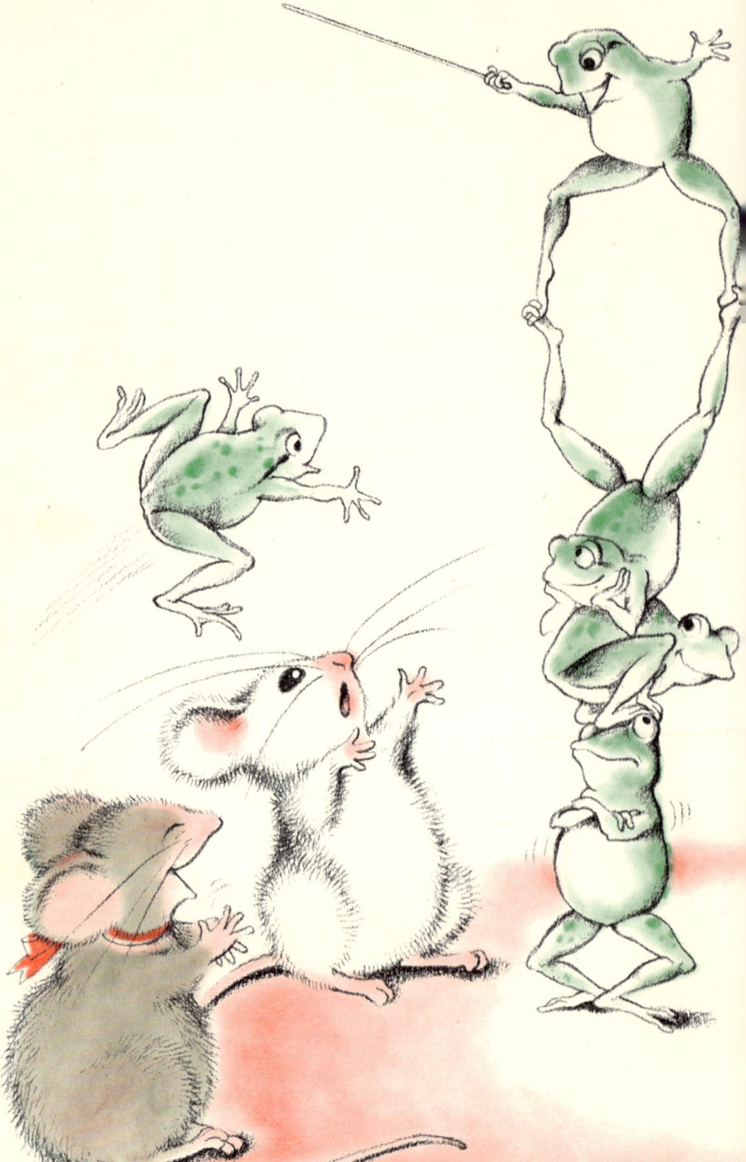

10 tree toads leaping…

...nine nuts for nibbling
eight crickets singing
seven spiders spinning
six wrens a-nesting
five bluebells
four holly berries
three thistle dusters
two silver pins and
a firefly in a fir tree.

On the

11th

day of Christmas
my true love gave
to me..................

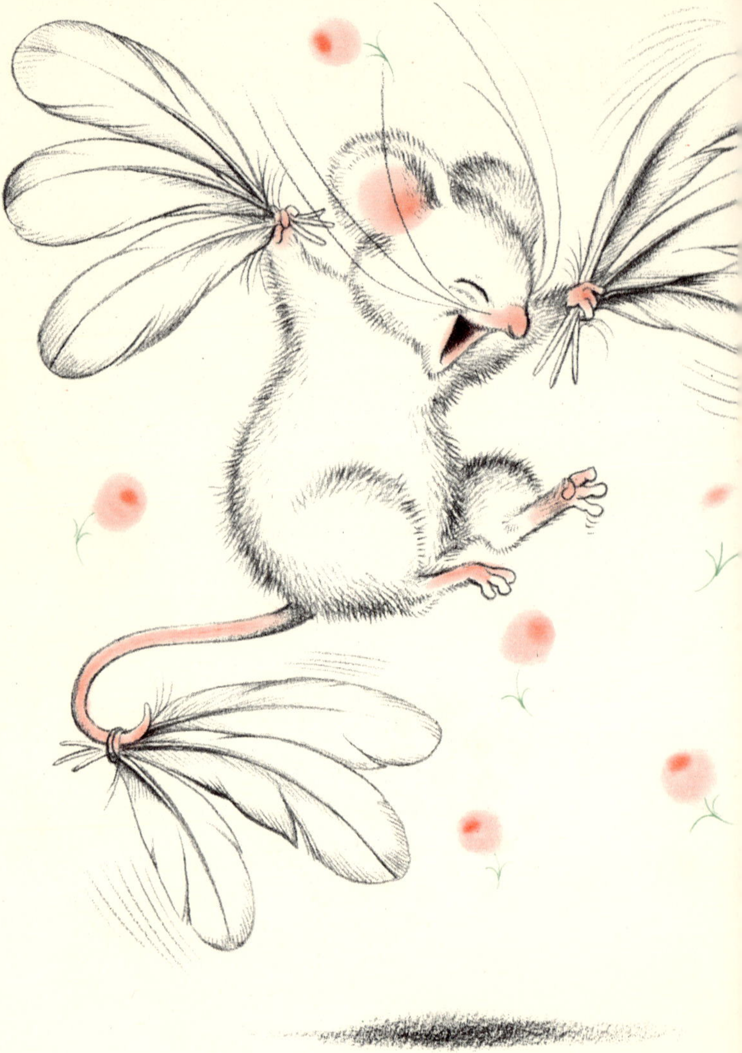

11 feathers fanning...

...ten tree toads leaping
nine nuts for nibbling
eight crickets singing
seven spiders spinning
six wrens a-nesting
five bluebells
four holly berries
three thistle dusters
two silver pins and
a firefly in a fir tree.

On the

12th

day of Christmas
my true love gave
to me..................

JOY

twelve bees abuzzing
eleven feathers fanning
ten tree toads leaping
nine nuts for nibbling
eight crickets singing
seven spiders spinning
six wrens a-nesting
five bluebells
four holly berries
three thistle dusters
two silver pins
and a
firefly in a fir tree.

The End